ALL EARTHLY BODIES

Miller Williams Poetry Series
EDITED BY PATRICIA SMITH

All Earthly Bodies

Michael Mlekoday

The University of Arkansas Press
Fayetteville
2022

ISBN: 978-1-68226-203-0
eISBN: 978-1-61075-772-0

26 25 24 23 22   5 4 3 2 1

Manufactured in the United States of America

Designed by Liz Lester

∞ The paper used in this publication meets the minimum requirements of the American National Standard for Permanence of Paper for Printed Library Materials Z39.48-1984.

Library of Congress Cataloging-in-Publication Data

Names: Mlekoday, Michael, 1985–   author.
Title: All earthly bodies / Michael Mlekoday.
Description: Fayetteville: The University of Arkansas Press, 2022. |
Series: Miller Williams poetry series | Summary: "'I am trying to make myself / a thrum of votive light,' Michael Mlekoday writes in All Earthly Bodies. 'I am trying to let the planet / rename me.' Through a kind of lyric dreamwork, Mlekoday sounds the depths—of ancestry and identity, race and gender, earth and self—to track the unbecoming and re-membering of the body"— Provided by publisher.
Identifiers: LCCN 2021053321 (print) | LCCN 2021053322 (ebook) | ISBN 9781682262030 (paperback; alk. paper) | ISBN 9781610757720 (ebook)
Subjects: LCGFT: Poetry.
Classification: LCC PS3613.L36 A78 2022 (print) | LCC PS3613.L36 (ebook) | DDC 811/.6—dc23/ eng/20211029
LC record available at https://lccn.loc.gov/2021053321
LC ebook record available at https://lccn.loc.gov/2021 053322

for Rossy Tzankova

I want to climb into their wolf bodies
and live there while they relearn
the world, deleting binary.

—ÉIREANN LORSUNG

I do not know what is happening to me. Everything
is green and shaggy and robust. At night I can hear
the wet grass in its dark ecstasies, I can hear the citrus
buds humming the small pains of their multiform births.
Surely I am not calm or wise.

—FRANK X. GASPAR

CONTENTS

I believe that all of us, every poet everywhere, can point to one mortifying moment of clueless ambition, when we decided that it was a snazzy idea to skip several thousand steps in our poetic evolution. After all, we were the annoying kids who bragged that we could and would memorize the entire dictionary, one page a day. (I threw in the towel at *abattoir*. You?)

Undeterred by the failure to master the all of our language, I once again succumbed to an unbridled zeal. Once I chose poetry as my way to walk through the world, and anxious to get down to business, I decided that I'd teach myself prosody and form in one big ol' fell swoop. Who needed classrooms and seminars and actual instruction? I'd picked up the enticing tome *Patterns of Poetry*, by some guy named Miller Williams, in the best lil' bookstore in Chicago, and I'd set aside a whole month to memorize everything in its pages.

Imagine—an entire *month* to master iambs, dactyls, anapests, pyrrhus, spondees, trochees and amphibrachs, as well as sapphics, the elegiac couplet, englyn penfyr, dipodic quatrain, awdyl gywydd, clerihew, terza rima, cyhydedd hir, rhupunt, and—well, the sonnet, of course.

This Williams person, whoever he was (remember that I was—shall we say, oblivious to everything except my own naked desire to POET), had gathered all that juicy knowledge between two covers, and all I had to do was sit down and pick it up. I imagined him on a misty mountainside somewhere, wallowing in wisdom and doling out prosody. I'd soon be joining him.

Needless to say, failure was my one and only option. It is notoriously difficult to teach yourself metrics because so much depends on hearing it from someone who's got it mastered and internalized. As Annie Finch—

the woman who eventually got poetic rhythms through my thick skull—said, "If you never feel it in your body, you'll never feel it."

It is also notoriously difficult to teach the emotional and narrative nuances of form. A poet has a dizzying amount of power when it comes to topic, perspective, and voice, and even more power when it comes to choosing the form that will pull it all together. As I like to tell my students, every single choice you make as a poet instructs the reader in the reading of the poem. EVERY. SINGLE. CHOICE.

In the midst of tackling *Patterns of Poetry* and failing miserably at both the patterns and the poetry, I thought I'd take some time to get to know more about that Williams fella. Whenever he used his own poems as examples in the book, I was tempted to throw the volume across the room into the nearest wall—they were that good.

I still crave the gorgeously stuttered music of the elegiac couplets in "For Victor Jara":

> This is to say we remember. Not that remembering
> saves us.
> Not that remembering brings anything usable back.
>
> This is to say that we never have understood how to
> say this.
> Out of our long unbelief what do we say to belief?

And this, my favorite excerpt from "On the Way Home from Nowhere, New Year's Eve":

> I tell myself I am blind. In such a dark
> I could be moving down the spaceless form
> of time, a painted tunnel. I twist off
> my shoes and walk in darkness. Leap.

Soon I realized that the idea of book learnin' myself into poetic prowess was a hopeless undertaking. But instead of giving up altogether, I decided to do a deep dive into Mr. Williams's work. I learned for the first time that he'd been William Jefferson Clinton's inaugural poet ("Whose law was never so much of the hand as the head / cannot let chaos make its way to the heart . . ."). I scoured the *Poetry* magazine archives, where this stanza of "For Rebecca, for Whom Nothing Has Been Written Page after Page" waited for me:

> When all the words are written down and read
> and even the creeping weights are written in
> what matters is what remains not said, not said.
> Which is what long silences are for.

And in his book *The Ways We Touch*, I found the wee treasure "Compassion," which urges its reader to shower each and everyone with empathy "even if they don't want it"—because—

> You do not know what wars are going on
> down there where the spirit meets the bone.

Well, amen.

After throwing his books against the wall in frustration, what drew me deeper into Miller Williams's work? The same thing that should draw me to yours.

I look for new ways to look at things I've already seen—things I'm convinced I know. I look for a hook for my breath to catch on. I look for form—traditional that enhances, instead of suffocates, its subject matter. Williams makes me jealous. He makes me wish I'd written it first.

And according to the man himself: "One of the best things that has ever been said about my work was said by a critic who wrote that 'Miller Williams is the Hank Williams of American poetry. While his poetry is taught at Princeton and Harvard, it's read and understood by squirrel hunters and taxi drivers.'"

In other words, I'm addicted to poetry that knows no closed doors.

It's been years between the time I first reveled in the words of this newfound poet and the day I became the editor of this series that carries his name. But both nothing much and everything has changed. I still need and expect to be knocked to the floor by a poem. I need it to hold me down, make me breathe differently. I'm a selfish reader. I want everything from a poem—and I know, for a fact, that everything isn't too much. *I want poems that vivify.*

You may, at this very moment, be thinking about submitting your lovingly spit-shined manuscript to the contest. If so, I have some pointers. (First of all, don't spit on it.)

My stellar contest screeners are also my teachers—I see in their work that they are dead set on narrative and lyrical impact, so I'm certain that the poems they read and forwarded to me have reached for that dual goal and achieved it.

But they also saw many manuscripts that weren't quite ready for the big time—by poets I like to think of as "feverishly pulling the trigger, but lacking ammunition" —or manuscripts that were enthusiastically submitted to exactly the wrong contest. The directive is, and always will be, very very simple: Read the description of what we want. Then send your one-of-a-kind, patented version of *that*.

In my college classrooms, officially "grading" poetry has always struck me as a bit of a crapshoot, because students enter at so many different levels with so many different ideas of what poetry is. I once had a fledgling writer pen a textured and lyrically complicated persona poem in the voice of a chambered bullet. In the very same class, a lovelorn student wrote, "When you left me, you hurt my emotions."

But the manuscripts that poured into the Miller Williams contest, for the most part, had obviously been sweated, prayed, and wept over, revised to pinpoint, whipped into formidable shape. There was a universal goodness to the mix, even if not everyone paid close enough attention to the type of work requested. But, oh—the top three certainly did. Each, in their own way, rocked the rafters.

Once J. Bailey Hutchinson's *Gut* rocketed to the top of the pile, it pretty much stayed there. Yes, there were contenders who threatened the throne, but *Gut* was always strolling in the neighborhood of the kingdom. It's startling and innovative and—how shall I say this?—a little bit of everyone. You'll see yourself here somewhere.

I really wish I'd written it.

But making sure it reaches you is definitely the next best thing.

Listen to this. It's the closing lines of "Ouroboros as Eight-Year-Old," one of the poems in the book about Bailey growing up with ADHD:

> she leans down to kiss the top of my head and
> I leap, I put her teeth through her lip. And. She
> holds. My mother's arms come around me. Even
> as I boil. Even as I pulse. Even as *spilled swim-*
> *bladder which is accumulated dollop of sap which is*
> *liquid which sticks which is inside an eel-bird inside*
> *a gas giant* which is blood on my scalp, which is
> my mother's exploded mouth, teeth two pearls
> in a red bed, *which is deconstructed willow-weeper*
> *which is a nest of purpled popsicle sticks,* she holds.
> Even as I become a jar of furious bones. She
> holds. My head a walnut in the quiet vise of her
> chin. Swollen grape in a lionsmouth.

There you have it. One of the many hooks I caught my breath on.

The sound. The surprise. The collision of phrases I thought could never collide. The current of love and trust flowing beneath it all.

What stands out about Bailey's work is her singular voice, graced with the ease and imagination of a born storyteller. She's a southern girl who sees no need to pound in that fact with a narrative hammer. She simply lifts you up and places you in the dead center of an addictive poetic lifeline, populated by cinema-worthy backdrops and people who refuse to stop nudging once you're done with the book.

The unforgiving edges of the poet's grandmother, Barbara, that "mean / sleepwalking woman" whose ghost "comes up from the river,   drenched in coontail kelp and fresh-mussel, // pale   as a goat throat."

Bailey's mother Mitzi, she of the wise and halting wisdoms, steps alive in the multisectioned "Became My Body, Too," stanzas of fractured and loving lineage. Here, a young Mitzi watches for her sister's seizures.

> At night, Mitzi would kneel by her sister's bunk
> with a garden-trowel   the grip all gnawed,
> (*how can a mouth   so* small   blister
>   beechwood?)—watching
> for the pulse of jaw,   the frenetic socket-whirl
> that took the girl's body
> before she became crack of cymbal   and seafloor
>   lightning.

And her granddaddy Hoyle—his ways with women and meat, his hard ways of loving—will be with you for a long, long time. This, from "The Butcher's Granddaughter":

> This body. Its rope. Before some pea-ball burst
> his brain, I remember Hoyle's belly—me, curled
> like a grub there, grogged on applesauce. He
>   smelled

like a good lunch meat, the biggest man I knew,
   singing
too-ra-loo-ra-lai through a mouth I never heard bite.

In addition, Bailey has mastered something I look for that not many poets can accomplish, something I'm constantly trying to get better at—when there's something she wants the reader to feel and there's no exact word for it, she conjures a phrase: Beer "nickeling my brain's-edge." A man is "shirt-wrecked by a midnight nosebleed." "Screwed to a scaffold, body-water glossy, / the hog opens like a Bible." A postcard is crammed with "cricket-leg lettering."

J. Bailey Hutchinson keeps introducing me and introducing me and introducing me to more and more brand-new world. Nothing settles. Nothing sits still. Nothing "makes do."

Thanks to this utterly original voice, my very first series pick is everything I was looking for.

Meanwhile, Janet Jackson (how's that for a segue?), who I go to for all my pithy wisdom, once said of her famously gruff father, "My dad taught us that there's no greater distance than that between first and second place."

That most definitely applies if you're a Jackson, but not in the case of Casey Thayer and his amazing second-place manuscript *Rational Anthem*.

It's hard to find a way to say this without someone taking offense, but *Rational Anthem* is a stellar *boy* book, pulsing with the triumphs and downfalls of testosterone, a muscled book, a book that's decidedly cocked and loaded. It's a book of men who drag their feet through violence. It's a painstakingly scrawled love letter to firepower. It chronicles men in their struggles with tenderness and vulnerability. It's the hunter and the blood and gristle the hunter knows. It's a book that not many people—certainly not many men, tangled in the roots of everything they think they should be—could write with such revelation and nuance.

Consider this, from "An Anatomical Study Concerning the North American Whitetail":

> You can love a man and find some shared action
> in which he tolerates that love.
>
> I slid my hands up the hollow muffler
> of the buck's chest cavity
>
> and slit the esophagus, cut the skirt
> of the diaphragm from sternum to crotch.
>
> Then I pulled the guts out. Sometimes
> I believe in small acts of kindness.

Rational Anthem often finds itself at the juncture of what a man does and what he dares to feel, and for the reader that's traditionally a shadowy and unknowable place. But Casey fearlessly inhabits that space, moving in the lens until we move from discomfort to discovery:

> **bullet • 1.** what thunder, teeth / in the threat, /
> blade in the sheath, / blood-letter bought / over
> the counter as easy as aspirin or an Oxy / to take
> into the body, / what the deed / leaves, hand
> that reaches / across the field, / snake coiled in
> the warren, / mole mazing the loam, / what the
> body carries, what is left / of the deed . . .

I don't mean to imply that *Rational Anthem* is *all* boy. There is much notable otherwise in its pages, including an unsettling ars poetica, an unstructured abecedarian that hits like a backhand slap, and cameos by Aquaman and an adopted blue whale.

But what *Rational Anthem* offers is crucial insight on how men think when they can't help but think. As the opening stanza of "The next great American elegy in the effigy of" indicates, the book is a deep dive into that riddle:

> you, who bonged from a severed boar's head
> Yuengling poured down its throat into your throat,
> who let the jaws of that giant clamp yours in a kiss,
> you, feral and triumphant in owning an animal for
> sport.

Casey Thayer's fearless exploration of masculinity is nothing less than revelatory. It manages to be contemplative and insightful, while packing a relentless punch. I will surely be gifting it to a few manly types who I hope will benefit from its bravery.

Since Janet Jackson never blurted any wisdoms about *third* place (my guess is that, for her father, no such thing existed), I won't be quoting her again in my introduction of Michael Mlekoday's *All Earthly Bodies*.

While Bailey and Casey do their vivifying head-on, with narratives that unfurl like cinema, Michael's punch is quieter—but its more gradual force, wrapped in a muscled language, still whips your head around. I loud-whispered "damn!" so often while reading this manuscript, my husband—the crime-writing poetry snob—barged into my office to see what was doing such a number on my head.

So I read him the opening lines of "Revolting":

> Even the gaze
> is a kind of government
>
> and even the outlaw
> wants sometimes
> to kneel
>
> if only in a field
> as full as a revolver.

And, just like that, he understood.

After the names of the winner and runners-up were initially revealed, I looked into their backgrounds. I was surprised and delighted to discover that Michael had been a regular participant in the poetry slam, the often-controversial competition where head-on vivifying is pretty much the order of the day.

The slam, aside from being a sometimes-chaotic performative arena, was also an invaluable training ground for the development of physical and social witnessing that brought *All Earthly Bodies* to this moment. In a perfect world, this is what the slammer becomes—a poet at the crosswords of resistance and rhythm, someone who knows that poetry's power resides not only in the scream, but often in the whisper.

Listen to this excerpt from the heart-numbing "The Night the Murderous Cop Was Not Charged":

> I want to know where
> all this weeping and standing
> has taken us, exactly. [. . .]
>
> Does the infinite static
> of the Pacific's evening tide—
> everbearing, acidifying—
> flicker itself to justice?
>
> Can the long memories
> of the pines imagine
> something like restitution
> for all the blades, blights,
>
> and wildfires we call
> history?

And it is Michael who penned that snippet I printed out and pinned above my desk. There's always that passage that steps gingerly from the manuscript to shake you into a new awake. Here it is, from "Whites":

But what is quotation exactly,
if not a way to wield another's prayer
and pretend it is not our own.

What language is not borrowed
machinery, echo of another's ancestors
burrowing the whole field of you,

blooming a grain you can't name
but harvest regardless.

—*Patricia Smith*

ALL EARTHLY BODIES

Revolting

Even the gaze
is a kind of government

and even the outlaw
wants sometimes
to kneel

if only in a field
as full as a revolver.

I don't want to be seen
for who I am.

I want to see the fantasy
that is my body
reflected back to me.

To sink
into the swamp of me
until everything gurgles ecstatic.

The ankle doesn't recoil
from the slither in the grass,

the blackbirds don't bolt
into seed,

the cockroach and the corpse flower
both abide their own
noxious beauties.

After

A bus ticket bought with an urn's worth
of change, three hundred thirty or so
post-binge pocketfuls—the odd quarter

spit from the jukebox like a seed, dimes
too embarrassing or precious to tip with—

will get you as far as Utah, depending
where you start. I was on my way
to Kansas, again, a dead six-cylinder

and a dead dad left in the wake of winter,
leather gloves the color of lemon flesh

blotted with crude oil, newly mine,
the promise of poetry bearing me
to that strange country of locusts

and tallgrass. I dreamt a bus like a vigil,
passengers holding candles with

paper cups around the bottoms
to catch the wax. If you try hard enough,
you can transfigure the smell of highway

into fried onions—sliced into rings
and crisped up, the kind we got

from the last neighborhood bar
and smuggled into the hospital.
My half-brother and his mom,

me and mine, circling that bed
in fluorescent light and monitor-time,

the mothers reminiscing about
the dying man's storied aptitude
for kissing. *Talk about a weird memory,*

I told the guy next to me on the bus,
days after the bustle of church basements

and burial. *Yeah,* he said,
we've all been there before, and laughed,
a gesture almost like belief.

City Kid Contemplating Wilderness

To be a body like a bodega.
Mouth begging neon from night.

To be made of elements and deli meats.

That animal art of translation
by tooth and tongue, lung and pore.

To flash mineral and mettle.

To become cat dander,
become tobacco duff, refrigeration.

If ever I felt unsafe,

it was not the wild that scared me,
but those who wanted to control it—

with nightstick or unwanted cock or money.

Especially money.
It'll pretty you up faster than a cop's knuckle.

Look what it did to the neighborhood.

I Pray for the Miracles

of refrigeration and ceiling breeze
to cease, for the machines to quiet,
for the exoskeletals outside
to come blues-up the crabgrass,

to cast some jazz against the smell
of leaves slowly turning to humus
(which is not, I have learned,
the blessed cream of the chickpea).

For my father lived
in the constant hum of indoors,
on barstools, and died in winter,
listening then to fluorescent

lights and his lungs
deliquescing inside him,
and I am my father's son
and trying not to be.

Insects, we say, once ruled
the world. Once. But I still
feel the swarm logic of summer,
the seats of power falling

as the temperatures rise.
I'm still praying for power outage,
for the city's drone to dim,
for the skies to wick our heat.

If I have, in disgust or fear—
or selfishness, wanting to keep
every drop of my blood
my own, wanting not

to become food myself
the way the earth does—
rained down destruction
on a million creeping things,

forgive me. I wish
I could make a music
of my body to bring
shivers even from kings,

or dream hexagonal,
or land just long enough
to make a policeman
slap himself in the face.

Have you ever knelt
on asphalt where, before,
your jeans had turned green?
Have you ever pored over

Kafka like a Gospel?
At your dad's deathbed?
His muscles palpitating
as if to throw off flies?

I am trying to make myself
a thrum of votive light.
I am trying to let the planet
rename me. I am trying to love

both the insect dirge
and the screen door's copper
breath as I press my face to it
and listen.

Pastoral

I talk to the moths and opossums.
If I were an apostle, I'd take the gift
of tongues and stick it in the dirt
of the only undeveloped lot
on my street, kneeling, to hear
what blooms, what bides.
A wild trinity of raccoons
pawed behind my bicycle for blocks,
one night, guiding me
through the dangers of the city
like a shepherd with six eyes.
We think this town belongs to us
and then a man phones the police
when a feral turkey corners him
against the brick wall of a bank.
Does it matter that it was daylight?
Are there rains that scare
the bejesus out of you when alone?
Do you just overflow with bejesus
like a catchment barrel not big enough
for the new climate's superstorms?
Once, I was unswarmed with loneliness.
I went back to the wilderness
to learn the names of my cousins.
I never did study the charts,
the hierarchies and removes and all that,
but I breathed the fig-soaked air
and understood enough.

The Night the Murderous Cop
Was Not Charged

I lifted a cement block
on my dark and drunk
college town street
and almost put it through

the driver's side window
of a parked Oldsmobile.
I didn't know whose it was,
but this was suburban Indiana,

so probably some white
asshole, I reasoned.
Then again, I, too,
lived in suburban Indiana

and I, too, was
some white asshole.
It took the years
and the redwood forests.

It took the fog's slowness,
sage tea and the smells
of bay, eucalypt, loam.
It took distance,

the kind afforded me
by the state and its taxonomies
for what it thinks
of my body and being.

I'm trying to catalog
how I recovered
the softness I dropped
on those streets

like, yes, petals.
Years, airs, invisibilities
the likes of which
are unevenly distributed

like, yes, sleep.
I have wept often.
I have stood in a mass
of human bodies

not wholly unlike
an ocean or organism,
beast or bristlecone,
a many-minded star map.

But living bodies.
Not the ones ended
by the same current
that keeps me afloat.

I want to know where
all this weeping and standing
has taken us, exactly.
My white friends

are, mostly, slow evolvers.
Me too. That's the thing
I want to take apart
with a cement block,

my own unwillingness
to throw the block,
literally, whenever
I know where to aim it

to bring back future ghosts.
My own intolerance
for fire. For penance,
and purgation, and debt.

Does the infinite static
of the Pacific's evening tide—
everbearing, acidifying—
flicker itself towards justice?

Can the long memories
of the pines imagine
something like restitution
for all the blades, blights,

and wildfires we call
history? My guess is no.
Could be wrong.
I choose to believe

everything matters.
I don't understand how
we live here. We hardly do.
But there are foretastes.

We grieve together the night
the rapist was elected,
the morning the unarmed boy
was executed and half the country

couldn't be bothered,
the days of evictions
and vengeance,
the days of empire.

We grieve with our bodies.
On the dance floor
I've felt my footwork
was mourning.

On the city bus we grieve
poverty shoulder-to-shoulder.
I am growing penance
like a garden.

Can I tell you what I want
with regards to whiteness?
Do you know how
a burned forest regenerates?

There are certain kinds
of seeds, apparently,
that only germinate
in fire.

Community Garden

There's a smell to weeding
different from cut grass.
It overcame me as a child,

playing at dandelion death
while my grandmother pruned,
or vexed the aphids, or preened

her flowerboxes like reflex.
I am become her since she left—
taking up her shoddy spade,

plodding frantic and arthritic
(spine, a quartz attuning to time),
cursing only what I love.

Satisfying, the cleanness
of a darkening patch of soil,
the uproot's muted trumpet.

Once, before, I came at dusk
and shocked a scrub jay to flight.
She dropped a chokecherry,

the thistles shouldered her off,
and I had to find the fruit
and toss it, lest it grow.

Once, before, I found a tarp,
a water bottle, a man mumbling
the bird-language of sleep.

I wanted to love him like a grandmother.
The shape of his shadow, of mine,
sent me back to the streetlights.

Another gardener overheard the chirping
and knew she had a tool for this.
The squad car came in the night.

I rend the bodies of Bermuda grass,
cleavers, bindweed, greening gloves
as I stack root and stem

to wither in the sun. Sweating—
they'll return themselves to soil,
and I will go about my work.

Self-Portrait as My Friend
Who Is a Narcissist and a Healer

The daffodils can go fuck themselves.
—JENNIFER CHANG

Of course I'm writing a self-portrait.
What else? The hummingbirds? The poison oak?
They remind me of me.
Don't pretend you don't know
that feeling. Once, you placed
the titan cone of a sugar pine
in the center of the driveway,
ate some mushrooms, lost your mind,
and said you were the one
who planted the mountainside.
See? At least I say
what I need: permission to be
a breakdown and forgetting,
deep soil, the trillion deaths
holding me up against the wind
as I sink and rise. Be a river
or pool of rain in a gutter.
You already are.

Interstatial

All night, the frost-rimmed windowpane
conducts me into new states of sleep,
while town announcements beckon me back

from days in my grandmother's yard,
fingering moss until the moss becomes me,
and I awake half-green, half-gone,

behind the slime-mold line towards
a gas station parking lot. The last time
I rode this route, in summer, we broke down,

as if a bus could suffer so hard,
it became a collective event.
Tonight, the engine is just loud enough

to paint a kind of privacy
over our semi-voluntary communion—
somniloquy, prayer, pillow talk

across aisles. I pretend a stranger's tone
is not enough to demystify their tongue,
and now it drifts into dreamscape,

Russian summer or Portuguese, their voice
turning me like the beads in their fingers.
We are animals chasing fresh water,

just one of the species of the spirit.
I sleep best with roots beneath me.
Once, I knew mulberry in the backyard,

the constant caucus of tallgrass.
Who's to say what's growing out there
now, underneath the freeway pitch,

so I fold a grip of dandelion tea
between sepia pages and keep it
at my feet. We all carry our curses.

Purslane, lane change. Theta waves,
the neural rhythms of navigation
and sleep, drag us to dawn.

The driver has changed since last
I woke and saw them.
Some movement in the miles,

peripheral—jackrabbit, or fox,
or some such ancestral sibling,
burdock probably riding in its fur.

Whites

But what is quotation exactly,
if not a way to wield another's prayer
and pretend it is not our own.

What language is not borrowed
machinery, echo of another's ancestors
burrowing the whole field of you,

blooming a grain you can't name
but harvest regardless.

I'll meet you in the weeds,
if you let me.

I'll show you scars
you didn't know we had.

As Above, So Below

Today I pull radishes from the earth.
We planted shards of almost-life,
my friends and I, not a month ago,
and now we taste the peppery

conspiracy of soil and water
to keep the living living.
Say what you will, the radish
puts the butterfly to shame,

its subterranean shell exploding
slowly into deep red, unseen.
Walking the sandy road away
from the community garden,

carrying the day's haul in a tote,
I look up to three rapidly falling
red lights in the dark Indiana sky
like a constellation dropping out of time.

They look like missiles, but here?
Can't be. If the sky was clean enough,
if the fogs and smogs of our hives
would dissipate for a night, maybe

we could see all the way to New York,
or whatever important place
where the bombs might be falling—
the capital, maybe, as they deliberate

whether we will shell another nation
of farms and petroleum. But not here
in the Midwest, home of fields
that feed the innocent and guilty alike.

I've eaten from them. I've paid my taxes,
cast my ballot, called it a good day.
At the garden, I forget to hill
the potatoes, I let my garlic scapes

run wild until they wilt. I doubt
the plants seek vengeance, and thank god.
But look: these red lights in the sky,
rockets or forgotten planets or hostile

visitors, must mean something.
I watch them plummet towards earth,
and I do not say a prayer, and I know
these lights are not for us.

Northbound Greyhound
Overnight Express

Winter teaches the four basic prayers—
grovel, shovel, glow, repeat.
Where I come from, January
transubstantiates the whole city—

even the high-rise complex
called the Crack Stacks,
me and the memory of Prince
leaning there against brick,

even the cemetery I used to
ride past holding my breath,
the cemetery that holds my father,
even the closed-down depot parking lot

where I once watched,
mid-route, a bus driver stop
to wash his hands and kneel eastward
and I almost joined him—

but we're not there yet.
We're in Iowa, its fields golden
even under deep freeze and dark.
An Amish woman whispers

her words for patience. Tonight,
I've got a window seat and my own row.
The sun is hours away, so I close my eyes
and trick myself into belief,

like the first and fiftieth times
I walked past the corporate coffee shop
that used to be a corner store, where
teenagers bargained for loosie cigarettes

and we wrestled an arcade joystick
so we could write in our initials
and give this sure and eternal place
something to remember us by.

Praise the corner store. Praise
the alleyways where I learned
about booze and black eyes
and open-mouthed kissing.

Praise resurrections and red dresses
and the west side of the city.
And praise the eternal bus ride back,
seven A.M., the skyline blooming

into view in the slow, first-snow traffic,
my favorite skyscraper glaring
so hard in the winter sun, I swear
it's burning to the ground.

Across

It's impossible to say, but perhaps,
dear reader, I have shown up
in a dream you had recently,
a bearer of apocalypse or grace,
maybe the words of your dead
grandmother taking form in my mouth,
or the moss from her stone walkway
around her flower garden growing
in my beard, all this through no
knowledge or effort of my own,
like a beaver chancing upon
a lumberjack hat, unaware, as if
the crow has no idea she ferries
the soul across, and, though we
cannot be sure—sometimes
we do not even know we drink
the dream waters—perhaps you
likewise came to me last night
and brought me just the magic
I needed, dropping it like pollen,
accidental as fog or fuchsia,
on your way to the hospital,
rushing, and without, you thought,
any time to give.

The Night the Owner of Our Second-Favorite Bar Put Ten Bucks into the Jukebox and Let Us Play Whatever We Wanted

We just played Prince and Tom Petty,
back-to-back, over and over,

and drank whiskey all night,
wished for a rain loud enough

to distract from the fourth run
of "You Wreck Me"—which was

originally titled "You Rock Me,"
until Petty realized the title sucked,

so he changed one sound and it made
all the difference. Tom *Pretty*

you called him, said you'd *go gay
for that guy*, and I said *Katie*,

you're a girl, but you insisted,
claiming you'd do *really gay stuff*

with him. You said it with conviction.
You were standing next to him,

then, on the stage we carry within us
like our dead dads, smoothing the strings

of an electric guitar. Tom
Purrdy you're calling him now,

your body swelling with desire
like your first acoustic in summer,

the one you learned on as a kid
until the neighbor boy smashed it

like in the videos
and you really slugged him for it

before running home to your dad
who was still there, then.

All this time, I've been backstage,
rummaging the fantasy, riding

the jukebox's repetition
like a ritual, gyrating in my seat.

Yes, I'm giving Prince a lap dance.
His bandmates once called him

a fancy lesbian, and I'm one
of his backup singers now, he says:

he needs to test my vocal cords
like tuning a piano with his tongue.

I'm singing *Prance, Prance,*
and I feel it in my spine,

when, finally, the rain rolls in loud
as the speakers' after-buzz in your head,

the sound of it pulling us back to this bar,
to these bodies, and I wonder—

if our fathers could go back
and change one sound they made

in our mothers' ears, would you be
that guitarist? Would I be that singer?

I don't know. We both shake our heads,
more to one side than the other,

as if to say nothing at all but say it
with grit and grace, and you order

another round of whiskey, and we wait
to see what song plays next.

Steve

A kid who kept a hand-me-down gun
in his backpack took a brick to my car window
one night and stole my stereo.

I ran out the apartment, shoeless in the snow,
carrying a baseball bat and a mouthful
of *fuck you*, but the kid was gone.

This was the '90s, the time of the coast wars,
the oceans gun-slinging across the country,
and we were pocketed in the Midwest

like an afterthought. He was my friend,
once. We sat together beneath
the spruce trees, but we didn't know

they were spruce trees. We might
have studied the stars, but
we couldn't name the constellations.

There's an animal need
that goes beyond den and hunger.
He didn't really need the money

any more than anybody on our block.
Just image. Birdsong. Belonging,
a desire the body manifests like perfume.

He could have become a police officer,
and I mean that as an insult.
I hope he knows I know it was him.

Scope

Bo pulls a cold McChicken sandwich
out of his camo backpack
and asks if I want one.

I got ten of them, he leans in and whispers,
*they don't got anything this good
in Afghanistan.*

We're in a rural Kansas parking lot,
skipped over by a Greyhound driver
with a full bus, with seven hours

until the next one rolls through.
In my memory, it is always August
in Kansas, the cicadas buzzing

like a power plant in the late sunset,
the air thick and wet with history,
Bleeding Kansas and all that.

I'm on my way north for a funeral
and Bo is just back from the war,
hoping to surprise his family

for a birthday or baptism,
I forget. After the bus drives off
without us, Bo asks if he can borrow

my phone, which I both hate and love.
I believe in being helpful to strangers
who grit their teeth

at the same stress I do,
but you know how expensive
a phone is? I abhor private property

as an idea, at least, and recite
an old Steinbeck quote to myself
sometimes, something about

the I vs. the we, and owning,
and freezing. I forget.
I spend forty minutes trying

to cancel the gig I'm traveling for
and find a friend to pick me up
before Bo convinces me

to wait it out with him
at the bar across the highway.
And then whiskey and the jukebox.

And then the old lady bartender
who lets everyone smoke inside
and tells stories about the year

there was an explosion
at the natural gas field.
And then a sweet hangover

of strangers, and then the best pool
I've ever played in my life,
three balls sunk on the opening break,

and then bar close rolls up
like weather and there's nothing
but an all-night gas station.

Some kids call us faggots
and Bo lets out a lazy curse
in their direction, says

we'll fuck you up, fuckers, we . . .
Then he tells me about the war,
about the six men he's killed,

how strange it was
to look through a scope
and see a person oblivious,

a person who doesn't think but knows
their heart will keep sending blood
to their limbs, at least for a while,

and is wrong. Bo doesn't know
I'm a writer. I wait
until he steps outside to smoke,

pull out my notebook,
and quickly scribble what he's said.
When he returns,

I feel like I'm looking at him
through a scope, the distance between us
something only I can see.

In at Least a Thousand Worlds

I walk into a fern forest and never return,
submitting to the frond hypnotic.

In thirty-seven worlds I die of thirst
in a week, skin brittle as dried birch,

jealous of the underworld's
long harvest of rain.

A hundred and twice I live
for decades longer, foraging mushrooms

like mushrooms forage the dead,
rising and declining by the season.

In another thousand worlds, I never leave
the city. There, I'm still spilling nickels

on plexiglass counters for chemical relief.
I feed my ego nightly like a dive bar jukebox.

I assume I'm rich in some worlds.
In one, I write a blockbuster

about all the hungry versions of me
voyaging the divide to hunt down

their monied and monocled twins
and bloody their driveways.

In another, I evict my mother's evictor.
Is it enough? Does it ripple the worlds

like guano does a garden?
Does another me count as me

if I am my own quantum sister?
Back in the forests, I encounter genders

vast as worlds: hummingbird, conifer,
Schizophyllum's gills like angel down.

I learn there is a season for everything.
A wood-guided wind pollinates

the many worlds with a single shiver.
A thousand leaves unfurl.

Quantum Sister the First

I crossed myself against the girl I found
within me, kneeling. With gin,
with slang and bad-neighborhood
vernacular, with everything
mustached and broken about me.
Still, I was overflowing
with woman names: fox
and wedding feathers, peonies
and plum blossoms, voice like syrup
pouring from me, the worry
of girlfriends my own.
Watch me remix you, she said.
Watch me stain your lips
designer red with sex.
Welcome this fresh undressing, sister,
this baptism by hairbrush, garden
swelling thick with the moon.

Trajectory

Raised by wolves
I learned to eat earth.
Raised by a bottle
washed ashore, as if aimed
at my hut by the sea's own
slingshot, a cursive message
rolled inside it, I rolled myself
to the waves. I was raised
by a record, spinning under needle
until my body popped and crackled
and people danced to me.
I was raised by vending machines,
and I excavated myself for quarters.
By rage, and I became rage.
By debt, and I became debt.
I was raised by men
but instead I am rising,
both skirt and wind,
to unlearn.

Dreamwork

Wild horses in a darkened basement.
The weight of vision in a woodstove.

The other prairies gauze-soft,
a daughter abandoned in blight,
just once they want the world

dragging the water west.
The last part of the body worth saving
and myself a series of mouths—

man, woman, boys and dead fathers,
girlfriends or grandparents,
I, I, I.

And then the timbre of tallgrass.
And floods of desire unchained.

Matryoshka

Is there anything but darkness
inside the linden tree
turned maternal doll?

Seems like a question for quantum,
but my ancestors had their own systems

for physics. They involved sifting
a palmful of soil
to count corn poppy seeds

against the shape of afternoon
arcing through the kitchen window,
kinetics of moths and nettles.

Dig down to the thirtieth doll,
thirty third, eleven dresses ago

in my family rhizosphere,
and find a carving of Veles,

the wet and wooly god
of earth, death, and cattle.

My grandmother swears
he became Saint Basil,

the same way she
became my namesake and father
when Dad wouldn't claim me.

Where there's need,
there's transformation,
piecemeal and permanent

as decay. The linden tree,
sacred back in the motherland,

produces perfect flowers,
meaning bisexual—
and who's to argue with the botanists?

Sometimes I wish I could
peel myself from myself
without discarding the shell.

Sometimes I worry
my ancestors would forget me

or send a *szeptunka*
to roll an egg

across my skull
and crack me into the sea,

letting that other grandmaternal
prayer sweep away
the woman I could be, some days.

I study the yolks in the mornings.
I do raise chickens, after all.
But I'm deflecting.

I never opened the nest
of nearly identical mothers.

They were lost in the move.

Echolocution

We trespass a stranger's walnut orchard
at sunset. The farmers here
work computers and stock options.

Hired hands. Shotguns for security.

Across the creek, we'd found a monitor,
trashed, an oak sapling rising
through the shattered screen,

the grasses claiming what they could,

and a small harvest of seeds
we carried in upturned shirts to the car.
The forest is a hoarder's orchard.

The orchard, more a factory forest.

Where I grew up, scavengers strip copper
from foreclosed homes for profit.
Here, orchards don't foreclose that often.

When in a wilderness at dusk, do as,

so we sound our way around,
siblings of bat and cricket.
We process being planetary

the way leaf-rattle does, the way of waves,

the way of frog city
and the nightly choral ritual,
croaking death's million names.

The wilds call back,

their song almost digital,
as if the farmers scattered their old modems
amidst the dung and dust of bones

to make amends.

Someone's faxing in the fields, again:
an owl, a rain dove, a red-winged blackbird
reinventing their ancestors' acid jazz,

a dead grandmother's whispers.

The names flood me like an upload.
Wherever the wires connect, I cannot say.
I hum. You howl. The elders drone,

chanting their old recipes in the dark.

Horizontology

In California, I find myself
stretching down to earth
like clouds unbecoming

as white women turn profit
at the yoga studio, seekers
and charlatans smudge

white sage and palo santo
towards extinction,
and I too burn what is sacred

for beauty or fuel.
They've always been
made of their own collapse,

the clouds, the colonists,
and I feel the forces
pulling me like precipitation.

I shed cells and spores
and whispers so fluidly
one can only see it

from a distance.
Even then, I just look
like a blur of myself.

How skyline of me.
How mountainously
I have eroded and crept

westward without notice.
How manifest.
When I say 'I,'

it's because the body
exorcises names like
splinters. Call it backlog

awaiting thunder,
or temporary home,
or tautology.

Let the body point
attention as far as it can
and try to preserve

whatever it sees.
If starlight, it's already gone.
Raindrops, too.

The ocean barely moves
from the airplane's
frosted window.

Plants disappear
forever and only
the hive mind remembers.

The full moon rises,
so large on the horizon,
so city-swallowing

and raw as gold,
for a moment
you can't even see it.

Ring of Bone

It's an old one, remember?
With the rōshi in the pickup
and the poet puzzling through
the countryside like a lone goose?

I saw myself
a sagebrush troubadour,
sporting skirt and six-gun,
fresh off the bus from downtown.

I took silence like a drug,
drank it off, walked sideways,
hid my vows like tracks.

Yes, the earth will take us all,
monks and drifters each.

There will be no boxes for the body.
The hushed globe will wait.

Third-Wave Animism

I have made gods.

The way the moon snaked
the streets river-like,

black marker and monsoon,
the stone-slow flesh of the animals
gathered on the porch,

the music they slept to
in the Old World,
work and sex and riot.

Say the night is an ecosystem.
Say the body is a backyard.

Say we are kneeling
underneath the feathers we found—
or was it moss, or haunches, or tongues?

Entomography

I write in the dark
a self-portrait in skirt and skeleton,

a line of me
following my own death's
scent trails,

the body signing itself
elemental, migratory,

dragging across the night
like a water strider.

The First Time I Wore a Skirt in Public

I watched a French poodle
snarl a hex and fuck up a pit bull
who'd sniffed at her wrong,
and I drifted back to my long-dead
grandmother—who had a poodle
when I was a boy
and I conflated the two,
the woman and the dog,
taking their ribbon and doily
for their only weapons, for
tepid water yet to be blessed,
until the woman, old world or otherworld
rivering through her to the end,
survived her husband (another breed)
a decade-plus on faith and flowerboxes
and curse words alone—
and here is this poodle
in front of me, years later,
growling the blood from
a muscled guard dog
and drooling it onto the sidewalk,
laughing, I think,
my dead grandmother's laugh,
levitating almost,
and I know it is animal in me,
this ungovernable beauty.
I wish we had enough witchcraft
to bring back our matriarchs

and watch them spit on the president.
I would shave my legs to the light
of a wildfire news broadcast.
I would roll eyeliner across my lids
as men younger and angrier than me
do exactly what we're trained to do.
I would sing to my face in the mirror,
my father's face, my grandmother's,
hexes and blessings
in a tongue not exactly
my own.

Such Leavings

Bad things are going to happen.
Your tomatoes will grow a fungus
and your cat will get run over.

But not so bad for the fungus.
Relax: watch one body become many,
muscle become a hundred maggots,

bone crushed to dust borne skyward
inside the stretching limbs of the plants.
Potash and nitrogen. Ounces to acres.

A so-called secular humanist says
the best refutation of God
is the predator, the parasite, the insect

which does nothing but burrow
through the brains and eyes of children.
Meanwhile, the deeply religious

eye-burrowing insect hums
lifelong praise songs to that god.
Here I am, anthropomorphizing again,

dreaming the insect dream,
calling on the moths with percussive breath
like a bard to the otherworld.

I, too, used to fear the planet.
But who's to say communion
shouldn't be a little terrifying?

Quantum Sister at Twenty-Seven

True, I dance like a man,
tinted and wrapped in split lip,
jawbone in fragments,

but listen. My chest is waiting
like a bird feeder to spill.

My cartilage is constant
as a neighborhood in heat.

Never mind the magic,
darling. Sometimes the snow
sweats clovers,

sometimes the whole earth
is one secret handshake away
from spring.

Milk of the wild—pulled
through the hum of my body,
the sweetgum of my sex—

cascades in spirit. I know
I will wake up mistaken for July.

The Maker, Misgendered

All summer they mispronounce your name
like warbles of air conditioner exhaust
in place of rainfall, cathedrals
built of apartment brick. The bishop's
lips glitter the grease of anathema.

Somebody protect the wild flowers—
singing the month of moss and slime,
kneeling the creek behind the cemetery,
praying the floods loosened like flesh.
A motherland from the broken body

of every father. Sometimes I dream
that self-pollination brings from me
the girl hunting the Mayflower sons
into long season shadow. Sometimes
I dream my name away from me.

Whose face gets swallowed in the white
of Bible pages? Whose face is less
swallowed than saved? If I could
see myself in fragments, I'd ask
the collagist to make something sweet

of my marrow. To be the girl apocalyptic.
Even now I hear the funeral song
flicking the dictator down the river,
the sermon storming under mulch,
the skyline slowly rotting back to bark.

In the Future We're All Luddites

This is the bitter blessing of the microwave:
that I can have popcorn at midnight,

smothered in nutritional yeast—which is
vegan for cheese and tastes like Jesus—

but it will be burnt. Blackened catfish
means a skilled chef; blackened popcorn,

less so. In the prairie days, they learned
to handle blades and open flames

by the age of eight. At that age,
I couldn't even whistle, or cup my hand

in the groove of my arm at just the angle
to make fart noises, let alone turn kernel

to confetti. Somebody reading this
in the future might say, *Why don't you*

get Lord Bezos to drone-deliver you
an air popper in the next twelve minutes?

But we're not there yet.
Somebody further in the future

might say, *I don't understand,*
my baseline quantum food printer

never burns the popcorn.
Fuck you, the future.

Here, some of us read poems on wood pulp,
and some kill animals for food,

and some of us really think civilization
is going to collapse, and soon,

and we aren't sure that's such a bad thing.
Forgive me, the future. I have watched

enough time-travel movies
to know you're blinking away

into 8-bit with every line break,
every plastic sleeve and pulse of radiation.

Even now I feel my hopes undone.
I don't know how we got the phrase

chicken nugget to sound appetizing, but
my mouth is watering just thinking it.

Crossing to the Otherworld

Let the nose-first animal in me
erupt into a field
of girl and good ghost story.

Let it be marrow and braid,
past as honeyed paws
and fear of my own flesh,

"them" as ripe cave,
mouth, fang, and spring.

Down, down, all the dead-swallowed
neighborhoods of the body.

Raised like a river in rainfall.
A haircut that becomes
the dozen dirts of drag.

Bury me brandishing
a dress, a pistol, and Poland,

broken as my lungs
in summer.

If I wanted the gnawing,
the sweet grief under my tongue.
If the cemetery expanded like a city.

If I was hard as the woods
and the congregation dropped

a letter like a guillotine.
If sex and exhaust be forgotten.
If you named me myth and nothing more.

Let me tongue daylight.
I'll be any kind of haunted.

Want

In the wilderness of my bedroom,
I saw a thick fog lift from my body
one night and take the shape

of a moose, then a man, then
the rush of animal desire. I was
untouched no more, my own musk

blinking off my fingers like rain,
my own fog my lover. My hands
danced a cave painting in me.

My teeth now fangs, my want
now black ghost and electric,
I swallowed the bitter hail

of the body and it kept coming.
It struck like a nightstick but sweet,
stuck in the blood like an overdose.

Maybe I took the whole flood
into me. Maybe the hunger
always has more than one face.

Don't ask why I stopped believing
in the body, my penance
like honey kicked from a hive.

Quantum Sister Never the Last

This place is old. Warbled altar
in the shape of boy.

A city so ruined. The draw of being
after dying. Our Lady, reincarnate

my father as a dress,
my mouth as fog, every saint a swallow,

every swallow a bat or bolt,
any kid from my block

one hot arrow into the river.
The body as a bridge, collapsed.

Come again as musk and moss.
Come again, haunting

the blood machine. Come again,
again, as a rhymed eye in the woods,

the smell of rain on sidewalk
the morning you left,

the body still bootlegging,
the record still skipping with praise.

A Prayer for Unbecoming

Don't be not ugly.
Don't not bark at the stars
from field or fire escape.

Pray like the rabbits pray.
Grieve like whale or redwood.

Get crookeder—
on the dance floor,
in the burrow or the hive,
the cul-de-sac or the cemetery.

If it be deadname,
take it to the midnight cradle of worms.

If it be pollen,
be it unpoliceable and winged.

Don't be not all that.
Don't be not nothing.
It's not not beautiful.

Deathwork

We can never leave—

flood water up to our knees,
organ praying its disaster music
loud as lottery or funeral Mass,

winter waltzing for the Motherland,

woods behind the city
collapsed like a cross over time,
April transformed into late summer storm.

Flame, energies, elegy—

the whole earth
eating everything
but the dead.

The Deep Hours

It is the month we mother
a broken-winged moth
with honey-water in a tiny dish

upon our bedside table,
a mulberry leaf balanced
on the lip as a bridge.

I dream of Whitman
in a sexy nurse's outfit

bending over soldiers' beds
and cooing, the old cougar.

I wake nightly, one body
among millions,

inhaling the sweat
of jasmine or moonflower
like smoke signals,

the precinct ablaze
two thousand miles closer to the river,
flowing sweet across the continent.

Tongue enough nectar
and the archetype darkens,
Walt becomes Emily,

Michael becomes M,
death turns desire,

the saguaro-sucking bat
crosses borders in the name
of birth and ritual,

and still extinction
reasons itself on.

I have committed crimes.
I have lived the fictions of the state.

Now I am asking the moths for absolution.

Now they are flattening their bodies,
wedging themselves
into the sealed jars in the pantry,

the great storehouse.
The asking is not enough.

They are showing us the way.

Extractive

Cypress sap dazzles my hands,
the kind of honey, maybe, that trapped
all those mosquitoes and mollusks

in the early days of higher evolution,
the late days of good
and permanent burial.

It smells of easy witchcraft.
No need to boil citrus peel,
rose hip, bone of rodent,
afterbirth, myrrh,

and let the mixture cool
on the windowsill of a full moon
in August. Simpling, they called it.

Just lay your hands on bark
and pull them back blessed,
baptism in reverse,

and whatever you touch now—
your grandfather's wrenches,
your favorite pants—
will glow like grain in sunset.

This cypress is young,
a hundred years or so
around the trunk,

though its shape of shade
comes to us from the other side
of the ice age.

It canopies like a baby's mobile
or a revival tent, a screen

our dreams will scuttle over
again and again.
When it all ends,

the whole stupid miracle
we've molehilled out of this place,

I hope the cypress lasts,
this one at least,
throwing its gaze

to the ocean, the stars,
and the mountains at once.

Vessel

Welling up with seeds
this week, the planet.
Fall is what we call it.
The question is how to carry
all this future dust
as the sunset shrinks back
by fragments, as the hands
unsteady, as the cosmos
strikes its squares and retrogrades.
Mind in the elseworld,
I pocketed juniper berries
in the parking lot
where I called the priest
for my father's last rites.
By medicine, we mean
a flavor to be overpowered.
No respect now
for the mellow bitterness
of mushroom, the biotic tang
of ferment, the vibrant real,
the secret sweet you can only find
after quitting corn syrup.
I vow to accept all earthly bodies.
Mine, too. My aching knees.
My back in need of trellis.
Like rosemary seeds
in your palm, I have a way
of slipping down to dirt.
Of course, any gardener

will tell you rosemary seeds
are unnecessary, for she grows
so well from cuttings.
Of course, rosemary
must not exactly agree.

My Love, the Creek, a Fig

Bruised and split
at the underside,
we take the body

of the fig,
halving it by hand.

Taste: tart, turned, evidence
earth knew about tongues
long before us.

Once, my love found a wasp
nested inside a fig,

wriggling and syrupy,
the size of twelve seeds or more.

Nary a priest has freed
a winged life from such a sticky,
transubstantiated prison.

Never has a father
found the host fermented on the tree.

We could live and die here twice
while the fig just goes on
exhaling sugar, ex nihilo.

We could, if we're lucky,
see past the world's end
as if through a veil,

or sunlight through the veins
of a palm-shaped leaf.

Love's lungs fill
like fruit

above the forest floor,
ripe with return.

Salvific

Every allergy, a purgatory.
Afterwards, I'm animal again.

Cutting the good rosemary
means taking from the bees,
for they know medicine better than us.

Their chants ring me monastic.
To tremble in secret means

fear, or want, or both.
I want it, the throb.
To fall away like a calyx.

In dreams I have smelled
the whispers of the herbs,
witnessed their heaven—

fields without end, air wet
and thick with hummingbirds,

night butterflies, those crones
hooded and yellow with pollen.

I have walked there with my father
longer than our lungs
would've ever let us on this earth.

Waking, I ache to return.
To go to the darker rosemary.

I draw the stone arrowhead
I carry on my person

and take, I think, only what I need.

"Pastoral": I just want you to know that the part about a guy calling the police on a turkey is absolutely real. There's a wild turkey in Davis, California, known as Downtown Tom who has been reported to police on multiple occasions. A real badass.

"Whites" was inspired by liberal white professors who think it's okay to use the n-word as long as they're "just quoting."

"The Night the Owner of Our Second-Favorite Bar Put Ten Bucks into the Jukebox and Let Us Play Whatever We Wanted" is for Katie Moulton and the Atlas Ballroom in Bloomington, Indiana.

"Ring of Bone" is after and for Lew Welch. It takes its title and some keywords from his poem "[I saw myself]," and it ends with a line from "Springtime in the Rockies, Lichen."

"Entomography" owes a debt to Aracelis Girmay, especially her poems "Self-Portrait as the Snail" and "Ars Poetica."

"Such Leavings": The first three lines are from "Relax" by Ellen Bass, and the title is from "This Compost" by Walt Whitman.

"Crossing to the Otherworld": The last couplet owes a debt to Alex Lemon's poem, "Mosquito."

"The Deep Hours" takes its title from "First Epistle in June" by Frank X. Gaspar.

"My Love, the Creek, a Fig" is for Rossy Tzankova and a majestic fig tree living on the banks of the Putah Creek near Winters, California.

The following poems are centos-style remakings, composed entirely of phrases which appear in my first book, *The Dead Eat Everything*: "Quantum Sister the First," "Dreamwork," "Third-Wave Animism," "Quantum Sister at Twenty-Seven," "The Maker, Misgendered," "Want," "Quantum Sister Never the Last," "Crossing to the Otherworld," and "Deathwork."

ACKNOWLEDGMENTS

Many thanks to the editorial teams of the following journals, wherein versions of these poems previously appeared, often with different titles: *Adroit Journal*: "The Deep Hours"; *Descant*: "Quantum Sister the First," "Quantum Sister at Twenty-Seven," and "Want"; *Florida Review*: "In at Least a Thousand Worlds" and "The Maker, Misgendered"; *Greensboro Review*: "Northbound Greyhound Overnight Express"; *The Journal*: "As Above, So Below" and "Vessel"; *New South*: "Quantum Sister Never the Last"; *Ninth Letter*: "After"; *Ring of Bone Zendo Newsletter*: "Ring of Bone"; *Ruminate*: "Salvific" and "Such Leavings"; *The Rumpus*: "Scope"; *Salt Hill*: "The First Time I Wore a Skirt in Public"; *Sewanee Review*: "Matryoshka"; *Solstice*: "Trajectory"; *Sonora Review*: "Interstatial"; *Southampton Review*: "I Pray for the Miracles"; *Southern Indiana Review*: "The Night the Murderous Cop Was Not Charged"; *Third Coast*: "Pastoral"; and *Washington Square Review*: "Community Garden."

Special thanks to Jake Wolff and Kenneth Hart for choosing my poems for the *Florida Review* Editors' Award; to Paige Lewis and Caroline Crew for naming "Quantum Sister Never the Last" third place in the *New South* poetry competition; to Aimee Nezhukumatathil and Aria Pahari for naming "Interstatial" a runner-up in *Sonora Review*'s poetry contest; and to Eric Smith and Paisley Rekdal for naming "Matryoshka" a runner-up in the *Sewanee Review* poetry contest. Special thanks to Jamaal May (at *Solstice*) and Alex Lemon (at *Descant*) for requesting work, which prompted some frenzied writing and revising.

Thanks to my teachers, mentors, and friends who have had their hands in some of these poems, especially:

Margaret Ronda, I Adeficha, Dylan Garity, John Howard, Katie Peterson, Ross Gay, Adrian Matejka, Jen Chang, Stacey Lynn Brown, Katie Moulton, Jordan Dahlen, Saba Keramati, and Hieu Minh Nguyen.

Thanks to everybody with whom I've had the good fortune of sharing weird, beautiful moments of creative community during the making of these poems. Ranjodh, KGB, and the cohort. The Bread Loaf Environmental crew: John, Lori, Anahí, Gwen, Michelle, and Jane. Sophia, Susie, Harlan, and Ellie. Trevor and Allie and Decker. Emily, Karyna, Dan, Alice, Zach, Kelli, and Ed. Jimbo, Sarah, and Dylan's parents . . .

Thanks to Patricia Smith and the University of Arkansas Press team for making this book with me—Liz Lester, Janet Foxman, Melissa King, Charlie Shields, David Scott Cunningham, and those of you I haven't met yet. Thanks too to Charlotte Bird and Marcus Wicker.

I owe much to the professors and mentors who have kept me on the path and at times made sure I had gainful employment, especially Todd Lawrence, Mike Klein, Elizabeth Dodd, Dan Hoyt, Mark Jerng, and Sven-Erik Rose. Shoutouts to my Jungian therapist Leslee Fournier, my Freudian mentor Omnia El Shakry, and everyone who has let me practice dream analysis on them.

Thanks to my students. Thanks to everyone who has hosted me for a reading or come to a reading. Thanks to my friends and loved ones who have given me shelter, hope, space, and encouragement over the years. Even if you are not in these poems, you are in these poems.

Thanks to my best friend, first reader, agent, and guide, Rossy Tzankova.